A Free Gift

I want to say Thank You for buying my book so I put together a free gift for you!

"Call Options – Bonus Strategy"

This gift is the perfect complement to this book so just visit the link below to get access.

http://pozittron.wix.com/musthavepublishing#!free-gift/c13s8

Contents

Introduction to the basics, learning and implementing strategies for successful options trading

Welcome to the world of options trading, a world of lucrative profitability accompanied by the complexities and volatility ratios that matches the payouts if you succeed. Whether you are a seasoned stocks trader or a absolute uninitiated novice on this topic, this eBook will serve as a non biased guide to help you familiarize yourself with the basic concepts, terms and available working strategies that are helping men and women all over the world earn a handsome income through observance, patience and flawless execution on trading platforms.

Options trading is one of the top activities for individuals looking for profitable investment and income making opportunities that do not require any prior form of experience, the best part is- the risks can be negated because options are free from the obligatory aspects that define common stocks and bonds, which is why it is so popular.

So how does one get started in learning the basic fundamentals of options trading without having to surf various websites to search and pore over the details while removing the bits of self promotion, or attending time consuming and boring seminars that you don't have time for , and paying hefty fees to a brokerage "expert" or "rock star" that requires you to fork out money even before you have made any for yourself?

The answer is simple: Read, learn and implement.

Getting started will only require a few short hours of your time to read and understand the basics and familiarize yourself on the inner workings of options trading. Once you know the basics, you are well on your way to observing commodities, indices, stocks and assets as well as market trends to pick out great choices, creating your own unique strategies, refining them and putting the strategies into action.

Is this too good to be true? Is this a get rich quick scheme? Will this eBook try to sell you anything?

The answer is a firm 'NO'.

Every investment or financial product requires a full understanding of how it works, the risks involved as well as knowing how to identify the market trends and capitalizing them in a calm and rational manner. This eBook is not a golden promise of quick riches, rather it aims to serve as a guide on how to get there in the safest possible way: through learning.

This is a repository of knowledge written with experience, verified and trustworthy resources culled from authority sources as well as the condensing of otherwise complicated and boring technical aspects to help you, the reader to grasp the subject in as quickly a time as possible regardless of whichever walks of life you hail from.

Who is this book for?

- Experienced investors and traders of common stocks and bonds or futures seeking knowledge on Options Trading.

- Non experienced individuals with literally zero prior knowledge or experience about any trading activities or investments

-Individuals looking to increase their quality of life with additional income through investment

- Individuals looking towards investing their savings to grow their retirement funds or nest egg for personal goals.

In this guide, you will learn about the following:

- What are options, what are the risks involved?

- Which terms must i know to be able to trade options properly?

- How does Options Trading really work?

- How to get started on being a investor?

- Trading strategies used by the best professionals and brokerage firms

These must-know topics are the very foundation of each and every successful trader out there today, and this eBook's contents will be the first step in helping you learn what the pros already know.

What is options trading and how it works

As with every investment related activity, it is never wise to follow others blindly without knowing exactly where you're going to place your investment capital. This first chapter will kick off with helping you grasp the entire concept of options trading and how it works, understanding what an option really is, and the benefits and risks involved.

Once you have understood exactly how options trading differs from traditional stock bonds, you will begin to see the possibilities of earning a supplementary income from this or to expand your investment portfolio.

First of all, let's begin with understanding what an 'option' is.

What is an option?

An option is typically a form of agreement or contract that entitles the potential buyer an opportunity to purchase a commodity, stock or asset without the commitment or obligation usually associated with common stock bonds or asset transactional practices.

The trader is simply given an option to buy or sell a particular asset at a locked in price on or before a certain date. An option, much like most stocks or bonds is a form of security, but with a different set of rules to trade by.

An example would be if you had the opportunity to purchase a prime plot of real estate which wouldn't normally be on the market, and you lacked the necessary funds to complete the purchase there and then.

An option may be given to you to purchase the plot of land at a locked in price of maybe 1million dollars, if you reserved the rights to do so with the purchase of an "option" of 10,000 dollars.

Now, upon purchase of the option which locks in the selling price for a pre agreed amount of time until you are able to raise the entirety of the funds to complete the transaction, you need not worry about the value of the real estate soaring due to high demand or it being sold off to another party who can pay the full sum before you do because your option effectively acts as a contract that protects your intent on purchasing that prime real estate.

In this scenario, should you have any reason to be unable or unwilling to follow through with the purchase of said land, perhaps due to a variety of factors such as a lack of funds or maybe you were presented with a more attractive investment elsewhere, the option which you purchased at $10,000 gives you the right to break the agreement without any ramifications except for the forfeiture of the $10,000 option you purchased as well as a fee called a **'premium'** which can be described as a one-time fee for purchasing an option(more on this later). This only occurs if you let the option's deadline expire without exercising your right to sell off the option, albeit at a different value than at the one you purchased it for.

So essentially, an option can be likened to an insurance policy that offers the trader some form of protection against contractual commitments.

Options trading exists for a wide and exhausting array of industries and commodities that are not limited to just real estate. Options are available for agricultural resources such as corn and industrial types such as oil or steel. There is literally a vast selection of picks for a investor to choose from. This would be especially beneficial if you have any prior form of futures trading experience and knowledge, hence making options trading one of the most versatile and interesting forms of trading today because of its profitability for traders that make good and informed decisions.

Benefits and Risks

In the earlier example of the plot of real estate, we can see that the most obvious benefit of options trading is the negation of high risk factors.

Due to the non-existent obligation on an option, traders are less exposed and vulnerable to detrimental events such as over evaluated prices, market downturns that more than often tend to cause investors massive losses or lead them to financial ruin.

Where the majority of investments tend to possess very little no boundaries on their potential losses cap, options trading differs significantly by offering a defined and outlined risk to potential buyers or traders.

It is *impossible* for any buyer to lose more than the invested sum (consisting of the option and premium sums), this is because of the right to buy or sell the underlying asset security at a specific price on a given date, the option will expire. This would then render the option entirely worthless if the conditions for profitable exercise or sale of the option contract are not met by the specific expiration date of the option.

Where are options traded?

Options are available for transaction on the following platforms below. Regardless of whichever brokerage or trading firm you use for transacting any trades, the options you buy or sell are listed on these main exchanges. Brokerage or arbitrage firms are merely intermediaries that assist investors in placing their orders.

- NYSE AMEX-(AMEX)

- The Chicago Board Options Exchange-(CBOE)

- NYSE Arca-(ARCA)

- NASDAQ OMX PHLX-(PHLX)

- The NASDAQ Options Market-(NOM)

- International Securities Exchange-(ISE)

- BATS Options-(BATS)

- Boston Options Exchange-(BOX)

This concludes chapter one of our eBook, take some time to digest the concept, benefits as well as the risks of options trading before moving on to chapter two. These very basic bits of knowledge are crucial in helping any investor assess potential options and underlying assets by understanding how they can take advantage of its expiration dates that correlates with the economic situation at any given time to produce a positive return on their investment capital.

The types of Options and the key terms in options trading

Congratulations on completing the first chapter of this eBook. Now in Chapter two, we will explain to you the different types of options available as well as the key terms or verbiage associated with options trading.

Learning and understanding these terms will enable you to navigate your way on the trading platforms with ease and help you to correctly identify any stock or commodity that can purchased below or above its actual value.

Types of Options

There are basically just two types of options.

1) Calls: The buyer's right to purchase an option

2) Puts: The seller's obligation to sell an option

Note the differences in the buyer have a right, and a seller having an obligation. Quite literally, the buyer has the right to pick out a stock or commodity option that suits his or her budget and with an agreeable or attractive deadline. While on the other hand, the seller is obligated to uphold their end of the bargain regardless of an upswing or downturn of economical conditions that may affect their asset's value positively or negatively.

If you look carefully at your picks as a buyer or seller, there is no reason why options trading should prove unprofitable for you.

The benefits of not having any obligations in a commitment or contract can work just as favorably whether you are placed in the role of a buyer or seller.

Call Options

A Call option is a literally a contract that gives the buyer the right to purchase shares of an underlying equity at a predetermined price, also known as the 'strike price 'or a predefined duration period (the expiration).

The seller of a Call option is obligated to sell the underlying security if the Call buyer exercises his or her option to purchase the option on or anytime before the option expiration date is due.

Put Options

A Put option is a contract that gives the buyer the right to sell shares of an underlying stock at a strike price, once again also with the aforementioned prefixed duration period. The seller of a Put option is obligated to buy the offered underlying security if the Put buyer exercises his or her option to sell on or before the option expiration date.

Expiration periods

There are a variety of expiration durations for different types of underlying stocks or assets.

American options expire on the Friday of the week of the given expiration month. So if you see an option with an expiration marked as 'September', then the expiration date will be on the date that the Friday of the third week in the month of September.

Typically, you will also find that there are lots of options which are valid until and expire at the end of week; others may expire upon the end of a annual quarter cycle or at other predefined periods. It is imperative to note and to understand exactly when an option will be expired; this is because the value of any option will be directly related to its expiration date. The expiration date is one factor of how a value or '**strike price**' is derived. This is because options are **derivatives**, meaning that their value is derived from and based upon various factors of an underlying stock or asset, which of course includes the expiration date.

What is 'Exercising the Option'?

It is key to remember this: the one thing that defines options trading is the absence of the obligation to fulfill a contract between a buyer and seller. Not only is this a defining aspect of options trading, it is actually the entire basis or point that gives this form of investment any appeal at all.

Options buyers and sellers are not required to buy or sell the underlying shares that are associated with their options. They can opt to resell their options, an act which means they remove themselves from a position where they stand to lose their entire invested sum selling off their existing option asset to others who may see it as profitable.

When an investor chooses to purchase or sell off the underlying shares an underlying stock or asset, the official term for this is called ' **exercising the option**'.

Now that we have covered the types of options as well as more in depth explanations on what goes on in options trading that included some of the key words and terms used in options trading, let us take a good look at the rest of the key terms or words used in options trading transactions. Why is this important? Learning these key terms and words will enable you to make sense of any interface or onboarding regardless of which options exchange, brokerage firm or mobile trading app you utilize to transact. No matter how they operate individually, they absolutely will and must use these key terms and words to communicate the pricing and descriptions associated with any option stocks or assets.

Ready? Let's go!

The key terms of options

Contract

This is the agreement between buyer and seller for a transaction of 100 shares of an underlying stock or asset.

Strike Price

The strike price is the price at which the underlying asset is to be bought or sold when the option is exercised. A strike price is derived from various factors in accordance to the underlying asset's attributes.

Premium

This is not a upgrade or more higher level of quality as its name may suggest. Rather, it is a form of payment by the buyer to the seller on top of the strike price of an option. This is a fee for the seller, due to the obligation conferred upon him or her for the risk involved in allowing the buyer to purchase an option at predefined value with a prefixed expiration as opposed to regular stock trading which gives no such benefits to the buyer. The option premium value will depend on the strike price, volatility of the underlying commodity or asset, as well as the time remaining to expiration period of the contract.

Expiration Date

The reality of Option contracts is that they are essentially limited time assets. Options can and will expire after a period of time. Once the stock expiration occurs, the right to exercise an option will no longer exist, and the stock option becomes worthless in value. The expiration duration and month is specified for each option contract. The specific date on which expiration occurs depends on the type

Option Style

An option contract can be transacted in either one of these two styles: American style or European style. The manner in which options can be exercised solely depends on the style of the option. The difference between these two styles is in the right to exercise an option. The right to exercise American style options can be performed at any time before expiration occurs, whereas European style options can only be exercised upon the expiration date itself. As of this time, every stock option currently traded in the marketplaces are American-style options.

Underlying Asset

The underlying asset is used as a definition to describe the security which the option seller has the obligation to deliver to or purchase from the option holder in the event the option is exercised. For stock options, the underlying asset refers to the shares of a specific company or corporation. As mentioned earlier in chapter one, options are also available for various types of securities such as commodities, or currency and indices.

Contract Multiplier

As mentioned earlier for stock contracts, one contract denotes 100 shares. A contract multiplier is effectively the number of contracts purchased or sold for an option. The contract multiplier states the quantity of the underlying asset that needs to be delivered in the event the option is exercised (purchased or sold).

In the money/ out of the money

This is options trading speak for "bought at a surplus/deficit" and "sold at a surplus/deficit"

Call Options bought at a strike price below its trading value is 'in the money'. Put Options purchased at above the actual price will be 'in the money' The difference here is between a buyer's right to purchase an asset at a 'locked in' price or predefined value because he or she pays a 'premium' for that right, and the seller's obligation to deliver on his or her promise if the option is exercised.

An example would be: if you could buy corn at $50 when the actual trading value was $65, your option is 'in the money' of $15, and the only way for the seller who sold it to you could say that his Put option was 'in the money' is if he had sold it at any strike price above $65.

An exact reversal of the above example would be the definition of 'out of the money'.

Options Market

In an options market, the participants in the options market buy and sell both the 'call' and 'put' options. A trader who buys options is termed as a 'holder'. An investor who sells options is termed as a ' writers'. Option holders are said to have long positions,

Long and Short Positions

A position is a label used to describe the level of involvement in a contract. Buyers typically hold on to options before exercising an option for a certain period of time which is measured from the moment of the purchase to the point expiration. This tends to be significally longer than the time a seller takes to drop an option from his or her portfolio.

Hence, all holders of options have long positions. And the writers of options have short positions. This may seem totally unnecessary or baffling to some, but these terms are typically used when an experienced broker or expert gives someone a tip or trading advice. The simplest example would be: ' Bob, go ahead and take up a long position on ABCD crop' stock at $104, you'll be in the money even before it goes up.'

In conclusion, there is quite a bit to learning and understanding the lingo used by option traders and the terms used in a contract. To fully absorb this chapter's contents, visit any exchange or brokerage site's market or trading place and take a look at the options listed and find the key terms and words from this chapter. Seeing the words used in live examples will definitely help you to understand them quicker and better.

Getting Started

(Accounts and modes of trading)

In the previous chapter, we elaborated upon the terms of options trading as well as the contexts in which those key terms and words are applied. Now that you have done your homework on looking at live examples on the trading exchanges that we also provided, this new chapter marks the beginning of the fun part where you will learn what is required to get started, we will then shed light on the basics on trading basics and what every new and aspiring trader should be on the lookout for when selecting a stock option or asset to begin trading successfully with profits in the following sections of the book.

This is never as easy as it sounds, because if it were, then everyone would just quit their jobs and trade options on a full time basis. What we will attempt to achieve here on from this chapter is to bring you closer to selecting your best picks for trading, as well as a few tried and tested strategies that have worked very well for the extremely experienced and successful traders out there. Instilling a sense of patience, a keen eye for ideal options as well as the refined strategies found here, we are confident that you will be well on your way to making profitable trades after trade.

How to get started

In order for anyone to get started on their first trade, an account must be set up and funded with either a options trading exchange or a brokerage firm, where all your trades transactions will be handled by and placed using a broker on your behalf. These brokerage firms will be extremely simple to search for and locate, and we highly recommend that anyone outside the United States of America to sign up with brokerage firms within your own geographical location to avoid complications when funding an account. Since this guide is meant to provide value and knowledge, we will not be referring anyone to any particular brokerage firm or mobile trading app as a means of advertising them in anyway.

Types of Accounts available?

There are two different trading accounts available when you sign up with any brokerage firm for an account with them. These two are known as **' Cash account'** and **' Margin account'** respectively.

A 'cash account' is funded with a deposit or transfer of monies from your banking accounts, and a 'Margin account' is for traders who already have a portfolio of stocks or other investments which can be used as collateral in options trading. For more specific details on a margin account, do consult and clarify with your selected brokerage firm as certain firms impose different fees when a portfolio stock is used as collateral for trading options.

What are the Minimum Deposit Fees?

Typically, there will be a minimum deposit sum required to open and fund a trading account. The specific amount required will depend on which particular type of account that you have selected, as well as the brokerage firm's individual policies on their pricing. In the USA, one can set up an account very easily with a very low sum of money or no deposits at all(depending on your selected firm) when setting up and registering a 'Cash Account' . Please take note however, that the Securities Exchange Committee or 'SEC' has issued federal regulations stating explicitly that all 'Margin Account' types will be required by law to place a deposit of at least $2000.

Do I choose an Online Brokerage or an Offline Brokerage?

The answer to this question is one that can determine the outcome of how successful you will be at trading options to make profits. Selecting the most convenient and effective solutions will aid you in placing orders without any delays or costly clerical errors, so please be sure to make the right decision that suits your needs best.

As with most professional brokers and traders we have taken the liberty to speak to for the purpose of this eBook, we have found that the preferred mode of trading amongst them is the Online Brokerage method. The main reason being that it makes placing an order for any contract far easier as opposed to the traditional offline brokerage methods.

According to the professionals we spoke to, it is in the best interests of the trader to adopt the online method as well, due to the numerous complexities in options trading that are ill suited to be handled over the phone (as many people still do with their stock trading activities until this day), the online method greatly reduces the risks of miscommunications between a trader and broker that saves them both time and any chances of making errors.

There are also a mass majority of brokerage firms that offer mobile trading apps that keep in line with the ever progressing advancements in technology that has been so closely integrated into our daily lives. Even this book is in the form of an electronic copy instead of the traditional paper and glue version, so why not opt for a seamless trading experience anywhere you go if the user interface is reliable and user friendly?

Fret not if the brokerage firm of your choice has yet to release their own bespoke app, logging into their main interface to trade will still prove more efficient and lucrative as opposed to having one physical broker who is weary and bogged down with never ending calls or in a noise polluted environment while on the line with clients at a time when you need to place an order. Having a fuss free experience and a highly reliable trading infrastructure is a priority that will help you keep your focus on the other aspects of options trading, so be sure to test out any brokerage's free trial versions' user friendliness before committing to any particular provider.

Effective strategy for beginners

This chapter brings us to what 90% of you reading this eBook came here to find out: strategies used by successful brokers and traders that are effective, simple to execute and low on capital output.

We've gone over literally almost every popular strategy available used in options trading to find the most viable ones best suited to new investors or people that wish to attempt their foray into options trading with as much minimal risk for you as possible. This section will not cover any of the more complicated or riskier strategies as those would definitely require the investor to possess at least more advanced experience and knowledge in breaking down the multitude of available strategies to adopt for their transactions.

The following two strategies are highly recommended and considered by many top traders and corporations to be the safest ones, albeit the potential profits will be capped due to the significantly reduced costs. This is a fair exchange in return for: **Lowered Risk + Simplicity=Success and Sustainable Profitability.**

Strategy #1: Zero Cost Collar

The zero cost collar or the 'low cost collar' strategy as it is sometimes referred to by, is implemented by purchasing puts while simultaneously writing ' out-of-the-money' covered calls. This cycle is to be repeated as often as your investment budget will allow.

The **key objective** here is to write the 'out of the money' calls at strike prices in which the **premium** fee received is **equivalent** to the premium of the **protective put purchased.**

The breakdown of the strategy is as follows:

-Pick an underlying

-Long 100 Shares

-Sell 1 'Out of The Money' (OTM) Call

-Buy 1 'At the money' (ATM) Put

-Repeat as necessary

So if you have paid attention so far, you can easily deduce that the parameters that makes this strategy an effective and economical one is that the output required for the collars are established to offer the fullest protection possible for your existing long (holding) stock positions with as little cost as possible. The premium output on protective puts you are required to pay for is ultimately offset by the incoming stream of premiums you will receive for writing(selling) covered calls at a price that is equivalent to the one paid out on your protective put contracts.

There is no 100% accurate method to calculate or deduce how much profits you can earn with this strategy, as the strategy involves several factors:

- **Investment capital**

- **Volatility of the underlying stock or asset**

- **Strike price value**

- **Expiration**

- **Number of repetitive executions of strategy**

However, it is assured that as long as an investor **strictly adheres to the given parameters** for the incoming and outgoing premiums, the profits are almost as good as guaranteed but with a ceiling on the potential income accrued.

Commission fees:

When calculating your profits from this strategy, do remember that there is always a commission fee to be paid out to your brokerage firm. The fees do vary from the $10-$25 range depending on the brokerage and your type of account registered with them.

Paying a one off commission fee will not decrease your profits significantly at all, but for very robust traders with higher levels of trading volume that wish to practice this strategy repeatedly, the multiple commission deductions can perhaps accumulate into a rather hefty sum that decreases your bottom line profit margin. Remember to always check about commission rates or any promotional discounts that brokerages tend to offer from time to time prior to signing up for a trading account.

Takeaway for Strategy #1:

Implementing this strategy is akin to the concept of forgoing any high level profits that result from a significant surge in value from the time of purchase, in return for tightened security (by writing the OTM Calls to) on your options value in hand that reduces the risks significantly regardless of the volatility associated with the particular underlying stock or asset you select.

We highly recommend this strategy for new investors wanting to try their hand out at options trading at minimal risk, but maximum exposure to familiarizing themselves with the two way contracts laden with nearly the whole gamut of key terms and words. There simply isn't any other strategy that allows new investors to start earning and learning at the same time while being safely protected by a negated and reduced risk, low cost collar.

We rate this strategy with:

Reduced Risks- 8/10

Ease of implementation: 8.5/10

Profitability: 6.5/10

Learn as you trade: 8/10

Effective strategy #2

(Synthetic Long Call Strategy)

What is known as a ' **synthetic long call'** is vastly different strategy from the previous chapter on zero cost collar strategy.

Synthetic long calls are used to **complement a similar series of long puts.** It is not a singular strategy. The synthetic long call strategy however, is **equally low risk as the zero cost collar but more profitable**. This strategy will be best suited to those who have achieved profits with the zero cost collar or those more inclined to use a bigger portion of their investment capital.

The synthetic long call part gets its name from the act of combining a long call position to work with a long put of the same series. Profitability levels for both positions will be equal.

There are other types of strategies that are also a variant of the synthetic long call, such as the **married put and the protective put.** We will not go into those details for such advanced strategies here, as this eBook is directed towards helping newcomers to learn the basics of options and strategies.

The breakdown of a Synthetic Long Call:

- **Long 100 Shares**

- **Buy 1 'At the money' (ATM) Put**

- **Unlimited Profit Potential**

The above formula seems straightforward enough for easy execution by a new investor. What is important here is to realize that this strategy, although simpler is much more favorable to investors and brokers because of the lack of a 'zero cost collar' type of output. More funds must be used to play this strategy to its full earning potential, but done so with a reduced risk level set in its place. So the less time spent on earning lower profits, the more opportunities brokers will have to divert profits to trade with higher profitability strategies and earn a better commission for themselves.

How do we calculate the profitability for this?

Below is a simple formula to help you understand how profit is achieved with this strategy.

Maximum Profit = Unlimited

Profit Achieved When Price of Underlying > Purchase Price of Underlying + Premium Paid

Profit = Price of Underlying - Purchase Price of Underlying

Well, the unlimited profits potential is very attractive.But what about the risks involved?

Have no fear, like every responsible guide we have the breakdown to display how such a strategy appeals to the best traders and brokers because of the lowered risks involved.

The formula for calculating maximum loss is given below:

Max Loss = Premium Paid + Commissions Paid

Max Loss Occurs When Price of Underlying <= Strike Price of Long put.

Takeaway

Whether you wish to adopt this strategy immediately or after you have made a profit with strategy #1 in our previous chapter, make sure you understand the differences between the two.

Strategy one: controlled and limited profitability with more protection on your stock's value with a much lower cost to start with.

Strategy two: Higher capital output as well as an additional ATM put position. Gives unlimited profitability potential in exchange for more funds needed to start with. Risk level is just as safe as the first strategy.

We give the Synthetic Long Call strategy the following scores:

-Profitability: 9.5/10

-Reduced risks: 8/10

-Ease of implementation: 6.5/10

-Learn as you trade: 8/10

The Top 3 traits and Must do's of the best traders

So you've learnt quite a load here from the last few chapters, everything from what options trading is about, the important facts, how to get started and even two really excellent strategies that we provided using information from our research on brokerage firms and traders.

While all of the above is sufficient enough for you to go out there and start making profits by trading, we'd like to really make sure you are more than adequately prepared.

Here are additional and highly useful traits and activities that we found most of the successful traders we spoke to had in common and attributed as one of the factors to their success.

1) Avoid the myth of low priced stocks as a sure sign of high profits.

In many cases, most new traders tend to find low priced stocks attractive by the reasoning that they can afford to buy more stocks if it is cheap, and that it would translate into more profits because they held more of that stock.

This is very likely untrue. Low priced stocks are indeed affordable and more attractive to new investors who are less averse to taking risks and those with lower investment capital. The appeal of such stocks is almost a no brainer to them.

In reality, almost a mind boggling 87% of such stocks rarely make a surge that goes high enough to truly allow a trader to amass large profits in a single contract. The higher priced stocks from more established companies however tend to perform better simply these companies are frequently churning out new advancements or services that improve their profit margins to keep the board of investors happy. And in doing so, large bag holders will very often monitor such newsworthy developments closely and buy in as quickly as possible at such large volumes that very often will cause a significant increase in the stock's value either upon the speculation of a big event or simply from the mass volumes purchased by news watchers that wish to get in early.

2) Always try to have a diversified portfolio

Diversification of one's portfolio is something that almost every investment manager or successful trader will advise you to do, and for good reason too.

Having a portfolio of just one particular security is considered high risk. If a sudden downturn trend takes hold of the market, your investments can easily depreciate or be worthless very quickly. Diversifying your portfolios is a form of risk management that allows you to keep a balanced and dependable portfolio of investments. The objective for diversification is to reduce risks on a overall long term commitment. So it is important to remember, although it is important to diversify, never spread your funds too thin by diversifying too quickly. Grow your portfolio at your own pace, and diversify at a level that will not stymie the overall growth and value of your portfolio due to a lack of available capital.

3) The 'Herd' Mentality

This ranks as one of the top factors that successful traders attribute to incurring losses or unsuccessful trading. Too often do we see and hear of people rushing to buy in a particular stock or asset because of some sudden increment in its value or news or maybe rumors.

In most cases, the rumors were true events planned or slated to occur as a form of profit generating activity by the company in question. This tends to generate a buzz among investors and 'hype' is built up surrounding the company's stock.

The problem here is, people on the outside use the stock's sudden increase in value as a form of validation to back up their theory or prediction that a big windfall is about to occur. A buying frenzy tends to occur after people deduce that the prediction is sound and backed by real statistics they see on the screen, which is interpreted as a solid prediction or a "hot tip".

What really happens here is that the true trading experts have already bought large amounts of that stock(which is why they are called large bag holders or 'whales'), and the rest of the average and regular investors that are buying in are actually snapping up the stocks that these big guys are dumping! The price increase (which people see as evidence of incoming price increases) that incites people to jump in is the result of other people like them who buy the stocks in a rush hoping to cash in on this windfall.

But in reality, all that frenzied buying is only profiting the big bag holders because they bought the stocks at a time when it was really cheap to do so, all that frenzied buying adds more profits to those big players before they decide to dump their holdings and cash out.

At the end of it all, it is the uninformed or new investors that get burned and left holding the bag once the big guys dump everything and cash out. As a rule of thumb, if you see even 1 decrease in the value accompanied by a sizeable volume shift of a talked about stock that goes back up very quickly in mere minutes or seconds during the "peak season", it is an indication that someone has sold all their holdings off to another party who was looking to jump in. If you are going to take advantage of merger/acquisition gossip or other hype related events that cause massive spikes in value, do it very early and get out just as quickly as you jumped in. The key is knowing when enough is enough when it is time to get out of there. Set a goal of how much you want to walk away with and never let doubts cloud your reasoning, don't get greedy.

Conclusion

You have read the top 3 traits that the best in the business implement in their day to day strategies be it for day trading or for the long term goals they have set. Go over the 3 points above repeatedly and instill them in your mind before you attempt any trading of any sort.

Many new traders bemoan their lack of intuition or knowledge when they meet with failure; hence it is very crucial to adopt the traits that complement sound strategies to further increase your chances of increasing your investment profits.

Set a goal and stick to it to achieve the end results you are looking for.

For additional traits and information related to the above 3 points, we highly recommend that you check out this eBook: "A Beginner's Investing Guide Learn The Strategies To Smart Investing And Start Making Real Money".

A Free Gift

I want to say Thank You for buying my book so I put together a free gift for you!

"Call Options – Bonus Strategy"

This gift is the perfect complement to this book so just visit the link below to get access.

http://pozittron.wix.com/musthavepublishing#!free-gift/c13s8

If you have 30 seconds, please
Leave a quick review!